My Refuge
Finding Peace & Strength in Uncertainty

Written by Debra Fredette
Edited by Mackenzie Wells & Stacy O'Halloran

Copyright © 2020 Debra Fredette. All rights reserved.

No part of this book may be reproduced or transmitted in any form or by any means, graphic, electronic, or mechanical, including photocopying recording, or taping without the written consent of the author or publisher.

Briley & Baxter Publications | Plymouth, Massachusetts

ISBN: 978-1-7350168-9-4

Book Design: Stacy O'Halloran

This book is dedicated to:

God the Father,
Jesus Christ the Son,
& the Holy Spirit,
my all and all!

~and~

Stacy Padula O'Halloran,
my inspiration & beautiful daughter!

Preface

Three generations of men in my family have fought in wars. My grandfather fought in World War I, my dad fought in World War II, and my ex-husband fought in the Vietnam War. One of my brothers also served in the Coast Guard during the Vietnam War, protecting our shoreline. Although I have never served in the military, I have served as a missionary in God's army, helping people in third-world countries battle the oppression of corrupt governments, illness, and poverty.

On my first mission trip, I went to Mexico where I spent time in orphanages – helping the people who ran them and loving the children who were there. My next trip was to Haiti, ten months after the earthquake in 2010. There were still a million people living in tents, and the week we arrived a cholera outbreak was spreading quickly throughout the tent population. My team and I were ready to help. Between us we had various skills: I was a surgical technologist and one of my teammates was a pediatrician. We brought medical supplies and were eager to administer fluids to stop the children from dying. However, we were not allowed to help the people, because we were with a church group and did not go through the government. Fortunately, we were still able to get the supplies to them. We spent the rest of our time in an orphanage, loving the children and helping the people in our area prepare for a hurricane that would be hitting the island in a couple of days.

Four days after I got home from Haiti, I was asked to go on a mission trip to the Dominican Republic. I flew to the Dominican Republic a couple of months later to do medical clinics in the bateyes (the sugar canes). Once I arrived, my team began traveling to a different batey every day, where we would treat 125 to 150 patients in a four-hour timeframe. After the long ride back to the mission house, we would make medical packs for the next day.

After this trip I was unable to travel for a few years because I was diagnosed with cancer and then severe Lyme disease. However, in 2014, I was back on the mission field and spent the summer in Uganda. This time I did not go with a mission group; I went with two other women and a five-year-old. Before I left for Africa, one of my dear friends gave me a card with Psalm 91 on the front and the story of the 91st brigade from WWI on the back. I prayed that Psalm every day, and God kept me safe. It was in Uganda that Psalm 91 came to life for me.

As a missionary, I have a lot in common with someone who serves in the armed forces, on a police force, as a first responder, or as a medical professional. We all fight against our enemy with the same goal: to help those who are suffering by bringing them hope and destroying the forces that are attacking them. However, we have different tactical strategies. A soldier's battle is more of a physical battle; they approach their enemy armed with guns, ammunition, hand grenades, and other weapons. Similarly, a police officer often has to use the same type of weapons against his enemy. Medical professionals and first responders, on the other hand, fight their enemies with medical equipment and medicine. My battle is more of a spiritual battle. As such, I approach my enemies armed with scripture, faith, belief, and trust in God. There are times when my battle could turn physical as well, and it is during those times that I depend on God's protection. In preparing for war, it is essential that I spend time praying for guidance. Whether you realize it or not, you are in a spiritual battle too. In the story of the 91st brigade, they also prayed to God, believed, and trusted in Him for protection. Rumor has it that not one soldier in the brigade died, even though they fought in three of the bloodiest battles of the war. In this book, I wrote out Psalm 91 and shared stories of how God came through for me during my time in Uganda. I pray that as you read these testimonies, the words encourage you and bless you!

My Call to Uganda

Psalm 91:1 "He who dwells in the secret place of the Most High shall abide under the shadow of the Almighty."

"I have learned over the years that when one's mind is made up, this diminishes fear; knowing what must be done does away with fear." - Rosa Parks

As I write this, America is in turmoil with the coronavirus spreading throughout the country. What makes this virus so destructive is that people have no idea they have it. Therefore, they unwittingly expose everyone whom they've had contact with in a two-week period. Those on the frontlines doing their jobs are risking their lives; many have died from this silent killer. If you are one of these heroes, I am so grateful for you, and you are in my prayers!

There is another enemy that most people are unaware of—he causes havoc wherever he goes. Like a virus needs to attach to a host cell to survive and take over, Satan needs an avenue into a person's life, so he can use them to do his evil deeds, or prevent them from doing good works. One of his biggest weapons is fear. If he can instill it in his victim, then he can take over a good portion of their life. Instead of peace, they will have turmoil; instead of joy they will have misery; instead of faith, they will have doubt, and instead of freedom, they will have oppression.

The deaf children in Uganda are called "Kasiru," which means stupid. They are considered cursed, have no rights, and live in bondage. Parents often hide their deaf children because they are fearful that people in the village will not trade with them if they have a deaf child. Just as dedicated workers today are making a daily decision to go to work to end the coronavirus and heal those who have it, I made a decision in 2014 to board a plane to Uganda to help end the abuse deaf children endure there and to find a way to give them the ability to hear.

My mission began in 2013; I met a Ugandan woman named Edith at a Bible study. She had come to America with her husband, Eddie, and their two daughters. Their eldest daughter was deaf, and they came here so she could have cochlear implant surgery. After the surgery, Edith and Eddie wanted to go back to Uganda to start a non-profit organization that would help other deaf children. Carrie, their daughter's teacher in America, had decided that she would go back to Uganda with them to explore the possibilities of opening an early intervention school. Edith asked if I would consider going, because I had worked in the operating room and had experience in surgical procedures. Over the next year, I prayed and received confirmation from God that I should go to Uganda and participate in this exploratory trip; so Carrie and I booked our flights. Everything was going according to plan until a few weeks before we were leaving for Africa, when Eddie decided to stay in America, because his daughter still needed some medical treatment. As such, it would just be Carrie, Edith, Edith's younger daughter, and me going to Uganda.

    I received so much opposition from family and friends about my decision, because of the dangers that were lurking in Africa. An Ebola epidemic had broken out in the west during March of 2014, and it was getting out of control; Boko Haram had kidnapped 276 girls from a school in Nigeria on April 15, 2014; and Isis named a Caliphate on June 29, 2014. On the evening of July 3, 2014, I was flying alone out of Boston to Uganda and landing in the Entebbe Airport at 10:50 p.m. Carrie was leaving earlier that day from New York and meeting Edith in Dubai. They were catching a flight together and were expected to land in Uganda sometime in the afternoon. The problem was, we were all in the air at different times, and Edith and Carrie did not have their cell phones. I would have no idea if they left Dubai or when they would arrive in Uganda. A friend at church had connected us with a man in Uganda named Adolf, who would pick me up at the Entebbe Airport and serve as our driver for the two months we were there. The morning I was leaving, one of my brothers called and told me to put on the news. The U.S. embassy was warning about a specific terror threat on the Entebbe airport between 9:00 and 11:00 that night. The embassy did not forbid travel to Uganda, but they urged anyone traveling there to be very careful. After much prayer, I decided to go and believed that God would protect me, because He called me to do this.

When I was at the airport waiting for my flight, I was being bombarded with texts and phone calls from people pleading with me not to go. I finally had to turn off my phone. My flight was delayed, so that gave me plenty of time to second-guess my decision. My mind was in a war with itself; one minute I was confident that God wanted me to do this, and the next minute, I was thinking maybe God was trying to tell me not to go. I called my best friend and told her what was going on, and she reminded me that God gave me confirmation in His word throughout the year that I should go. That was all I needed to hear. When it came time to board the plane, my heart was beating so fast. I was terrified! I knew, however, that it was Satan who did not want me to help the deaf children in Africa and that fear was from him, not God. I boarded the plane, and once I sat down in my seat, I had such a peace. The definition of the word "abide" is to "accept or act in accordance with (a rule, decision, or recommendation)." I accepted my mission from God, so I guess you could say that I was "<u>abiding under the shadow of the Almighty</u>," as is stated in Psalm 91:1.

Reflection

Just as someone in the armed forces trusts their commanding officer to provide cover for them when they are in combat, I have faith that God will provide a shield over me when I am on the battlefield. Knowing that someone "has your back" as you venture out makes a difference in your level of fear and your decision to move forward. It is important to remember where fear comes from, and that *you* decide whether to let it in or to reject it. If you had a choice to allow the coronavirus into your body or reject it, what would you do? I believe you would do everything to block its entrance because of its destructive capabilities. Fearfulness causes devastation as well—it can paralyze you and prevent you from pursuing your dreams. It also keeps you from experiencing life to its fullest.

If you are stepping out into some unknown place right now, perhaps it's a new profession or some other unchartered territory, who do you rely on for reassurance or backup when your plan fails? The following words, from my commander and chief, give me confidence and peace to go forward when I am battling fear:

"I can do all things through Christ who strengthens me" - Philippians 4:13

"Be anxious for nothing, but in everything by prayer and supplication, with thanksgiving, let your requests be made known to God; and the peace of God, which surpasses all understanding, will guard your hearts and minds through Christ Jesus" - Philippians 4:6-7

The Flight

Psalm 91:2 "I will say of the Lord, <u>He is my refuge and my fortress</u>; <u>my God</u>, <u>in Him I will trust</u>."

"The brave man is not he who does not feel afraid, but he who conquers that fear" - Nelson Mandela

Foreign territory does not have to be an actual place; it can be a situation that we have never encountered before, and we have no idea how to deal with it. Perhaps, it's a virus that we know nothing about, or an economy that seems to be crashing. These things are out of our control; however, we still have to deal with them. When I boarded my plane in London, I did not expect to sit next someone who would paint a grim picture of what I could face when I landed in Uganda. Although it may have been realistic, it got my eyes off God and my mission and onto myself. Be careful of those who fuel the fire of fear. Once you have decided to step out in faith, the enemy of your soul will try to get you off track.

I was flying from Boston to London and then on to Uganda. I had flown into Heathrow Airport a few times, so I was not nervous about finding my way to the gate for my connecting flight. However, I *was* nervous about making the connecting flight in time, because my flight out of Boston was delayed so long. When I landed in London, I had to go through customs again and literally run to my connecting flight—I was the last one to board the plane to Uganda. After my plane took off, I read for a while and then nodded off.

When I woke up, I started talking to the man beside me; his name was Wally. He asked what organization I was with. I told him I was not with an organization and explained the situation.

He said, "I run a ministry and come here every year with a group of people. We do healing services and there are thousands of people that come to our revivals. What are you going to do if your friends didn't make it to Uganda and your driver doesn't show up?"

I told him that my family made me book a room at the Sheraton Hotel in Kampala, and I would go there.

He said, "It is not safe to be out at night in Kampala. You can't get into a cab at midnight to go to your hotel. People will never see you again."

I was starting to feel sick to my stomach; it may have been a combination of fear and the fact that I forgot to book a gluten-free meal—all I had eaten for eight hours was a salad. I went to the bathroom and started praying. I asked God to help me; then I went back to my seat. Since the pastor did healing services, I asked him if he could pray for my stomach to feel better. After he prayed, I thanked him and put my earplugs in to listen to Christian music. I could not talk to him anymore—he was scaring the daylights out of me! As we were getting closer to landing, I asked him who was picking his group up and where they were staying.

He said, "A van is picking us up, and there is a guy on the van with a gun. We are going to spend the night at a mission house that has a gate and wall around it, and there are armed guards at the gate."

I asked him if I could spend the night with his group if my driver didn't show up. He thought about it for a minute and then said yes.

When we landed in Uganda at 10:50 p.m. and we were walking towards customs, there was a problem with someone in Wally's group. I was afraid to wait with them—If my driver and the girls were there to pick me up and I did not walk out of the airport shortly after I landed, they may leave, thinking that I missed my connecting flight. Therefore, I went through customs; however, I had no idea where to go to get my luggage. There was a mission couple with their two children walking near me. I asked them where I needed to go, and they told me to walk with them. Their luggage came out before mine, and they left. As I waited for my luggage, another mission couple approached me and asked me if I was alone. I said yes, and they said they would walk out of the airport with me. God certainly put people in my path to help me; He is so faithful!! I got my luggage, and I waited a while, but the couple with me still did not have their luggage; I told them that I was going to go outside. As I walked away the following scripture came to my mind, "God has not given us a spirit of fear, but of power and of love and of a sound mind (2 Timothy 1:7). When I walked out the door to leave the airport, I felt someone hug my legs. It was Edith's five-year-old daughter. The girls were there to meet me! By the time we got to the house we were renting and got into bed, it was 3:30am. I was exhausted but so thankful to God. <u>He was my refuge, my</u> <u>fortress</u>. I blocked out what everybody had said to me all day and night, and <u>I put my trust in Him alone</u>; God came through for me, just as He promised in Psalm 91:2.

Reflection

Some people are planners and have a peace knowing that they have done everything possible for things to go smoothly; this is actually a form of control. Others can easily set out on a journey without any plans or expectations. Either way, there is still a chance that a situation will transpire that you never expected to happen. On the plane I was told that I could not safely go to the hotel I had booked in case the girls and my driver were not there to pick me up. However, I still made a choice to leave Wally and his group and walk out of the airport alone. I was able to do this because my faith was not in my plan, but in God's plan. My trust was in His ability—not my own—to work things together for good. If you find yourself in this type of dilemma and your only choice is to keep moving forward, how will you successfully do this? I'm not talking about a life and death decision where your adrenaline kicks in and takes over. I am talking about a situation when a journey has come to an end—maybe it is a relationship or a career. When your plan fails, who or what do you put your trust and faith in to get you through this predicament? When I was a child, I knew that my dad loved me and would do whatever he could to help me and, therefore, I trusted him. The reason I can put my trust in God is because I know how much he loves me and unlike my dad, He *can* do all things. Below are the words that my Heavenly Father spoke to one of His children a long time ago. I know these words are for me and for you as well:

"Fear not, for I am with you; be not dismayed, for I am your God. I will strengthen you, yes I will help you, I will uphold you with My righteous right hand" - Isaiah 41:10

"I will instruct you and teach you in the way you should go; I will guide you with My eye" - Psalm 32:8

Sipi Falls

Psalm 91:3 "Surely <u>He shall deliver you from the snare of the fowler</u> and from the perilous pestilence."

"Faith never knows where it is being led, but it loves and knows the One who is leading" - Oswald Chambers

There are all kinds of unknowns in the world: plagues, scams, and fraud. It can be a very scary place to live in at times. With all the invisible bacteria and deception, it is hard to know whom to believe or trust. We cannot see the pathogens inside us or the people's hearts around us, so we often have to depend on our instinct. Have you wondered where this intuition comes from?

We spent our first few days in Uganda visiting schools for the deaf in Kampala. On our fifth day, we traveled to eastern Uganda. Edith said we needed to get to Mbale before dark, because some of the roads were not safe to travel on at night. Our driver, Adolf, was not feeling well and was a little late picking us up, so we did not get on the road until 1:30 p.m. By the time we got to Mbale it was dark, but <u>God protected us.</u>

We spent one and a half days visiting the CURE Children's Hospital, which specializes in Neurosurgery. When we left the hospital to go to another location, we decided to stop on our way and hike Sipi Falls in Kapchorwa. As we were looking for the falls, we stopped at a scenic sight to take some pictures. A man named Mike was riding a motorcycle past the site. He stopped and told us that he was a tour guide, and we should hire him to take us to the falls. We were skeptical, but we followed him to a charming resort where the trail began. I still did not have a peace about it, so we prayed before we started our hike. We climbed a trail that was barely a foot wide with thick bushes on both sides. I am afraid of snakes, and before I landed in Uganda, I prayed that I would not see any. The trail had lots of rocks, and it was a little slippery. About halfway up the trail, we stopped near a cave. We were actually underneath part of the falls, and the power of the water was amazing. As we walked back down the trail, I talked with

Mike. He told me stories about men crossing the nearby Kenyan border and killing parents, which left many orphan children. We also talked about various topics in America and in Uganda. He asked if I was on vacation, and I explained why I was in Africa.

Next, we hiked to a cave with an ominous atmosphere. Although I did not venture too far inside, I saw where animals lived and where ceremonies took place. When a man suddenly appeared, Mike began talking to him. The sound of motorcycles in the distance gave me an uneasy feeling because we were in the middle of the woods; I felt as though the Holy Spirit was prompting me to flee the area.

"We have to head back now!" I cried, while rapidly exiting the cave and hustling down the path.

After a short delay, the rest of the group followed me. At the bottom of the hill, Mike suggested that we drive to a nearby trail where we could view the falls from above. Despite everyone else's enthusiasm, I still had a check in my spirit. My apprehension continued to grow when we reached our vehicle. Adolf, who was inspecting the tires, said he feared someone could tamper with them.

We got in our car and followed Mike up the street and down a long dirt driveway. When we got to the end, there were some men trimming bushes. I had an unsettled feeling, but I did notice a resort behind the workers. The grounds were beautiful, and as we began walking, the falls were to our right. The scenery was breath taking! Mike continued to talk to me as we walked. We decided to give him a good tip because he was a great tour guide.

When we got back to the car, one of the tires was almost completely flat. Obviously, someone let the air out of the tire. The guys who were working on the bushes just kept staring at us. My mind was in turmoil. "We are in the middle of nowhere! We cannot drive far with a flat tire and why are these guys staring at us? Are they trying to figure out how to attack us?" My thoughts were interrupted when Mike said, "follow me, I will show you where you can get some air for your tire." We had no choice but to follow him and trust God to deliver us. I thought we could be getting set up to be robbed—or even worse, so I started praying out loud that God would keep us safe and get us some air for the tire. We drove to the nearest village where Mike pulled in front of a building. There were men in front of the building and a group of men across the street who walked over to us. Adolf and Edith got out of the car and told us to stay in the car. I saw Mike look at the men and shake his head no. He got on his bike and left. I was nervous but was trusting God to help us. Mike came back shortly with a guest book for us to sign while one of the men began filling up our tire with an air pump. Once our tire was full, we left. I still believe that their original plan was to rob us, but Mike did not allow it because he got to know us. Of course I cannot be sure about that, but what I am sure of is that God kept us safe <u>from the snare of the fowler</u>, as it says in Psalm 91:3. With all the hiking in the woods, I didn't see one snake. God answered all my prayers!!

Reflection

Since there is such uncertainty in the world, we never know when we may find ourselves in trouble. My feeling throughout the day was to be on guard. Have you ever been lost and had no idea which way to go, so you followed your gut and it was the right way to get you to your destination? What prompted that impulse? Scientist believe that animals have instinct embedded in their brain—my question is... who put it there? Why do animals and some people have it? I believe that all things were created by God and that it is the Holy Spirit warning and guiding. The words below guide and empower me when I find myself in harm's way:

"Whether you turn to the right or to the left, your ears will hear a voice behind you saying this is the way; walk in it" - Isaiah 30:21.

"When He, the Spirit of truth has come, He will guide you into all truth; for He will not speak on His own authority, but whatever He hears He will speak; and He will tell you things to come" John 16:13

The Back Gate

Psalm 91:4 "He shall cover you with His feathers, and <u>under His wings you shall take refuge;</u> <u>His truth shall be your shield and buckler.</u>"

"Do not begin to measure your safety by your comfort—but measure it by the eternal word of God, which you have believed and which you know to be true" - Charles Spurgeon

Some of us find comfort knowing our doors are locked, and our security system will sound an alarm if an intruder enters the house. If we profess that God is our protector, do we really believe that? The first time I read Psalm 91:4, I had to look up what a buckler was. It is shield used in hand-to-hand combat. So, this scripture tells me that I can take shelter under God's everlasting arms when I need protection, and He will shield, protect, and fight for me. It also says, "He will cover me with His feathers." What or whom do you trust to be your protector?

The house we were renting for the summer was on the outskirts of Kampala in a poor Muslim neighborhood. One of the reasons we rented this house was because it had a wall around it with barbed wire on the top and a locked front gate, which a man named Charles would open and close as we came in and out. There were two other houses behind this wall that Ugandan families lived in. Our backyard had a rope that went from a rod to a tree for our clothesline. There was also a locked gate in the backyard, which led to another Muslim neighborhood.

Every time we got back from days of traveling, we had to wash our clothes by hand in a tub or sink. One day Edith was visiting her mom while Carrie and I were at the house doing laundry. I went outside to hang my wet clothes on the line. Suddenly, the back gate opened and two big men started walking in my direction. I said hello, but they gave no reply and just kept walking toward me. Then I softly said two words: Jesus help! The men walked up to me, but then passed right by me, as if they did not even see me there. I ran into our house and told Carrie to lock the doors and shut the windows. The guys walked around the side of our house and then into the house next to us.

  After the men left that house, we went over to talk to our neighbor. We asked him why the back gate was not locked. He told us they never lock the gate because their children go out into the neighborhood to play, and he would have to give them all keys. Carrie and I explained that we rented the house because of the safety precautions and that we wanted the gate locked. He told us that he would have keys made for the children in both of the houses. A couple of weeks went by, but the gate was still unlocked, and the children had no keys. Carrie and I debated about talking to our neighbor again, but then we realized that the locked gate was not protecting us— God was protecting us. We had been in Uganda for a few weeks, and the gate had been unlocked the whole time, with no incident. We told our neighbor that he did not have to make keys for the children. <u>God was and is my shield and buckler—I took refuge under His wings,</u> as Psalm 91:4 promises, and He fulfilled His promise.

Reflection

  I do not know why I felt that I needed a locked gate to protect me. The creator of Heaven and Earth has promised to be a refuge for me, and yet I still felt the need to have the gate secured. Sometimes criminals still find a way into a house that has every type of security device. Who or what is your guarantee for safety? As human beings we protect the people and things we value. God's word says, "For where your treasure is, there your heart will be also" (Matthew 6:21). Since God sent His son Jesus to die for me, I'm pretty sure he thinks I am valuable. Therefore, I choose to put my faith in God.The words below encourage and keep me calm when I feel vulnerable:

"You will keep him in perfect peace, whose mind is stayed on You Because he trusts in You" - Isaiah 26:3

"You are my hiding place; You shall preserve me from trouble; You shall surround me with songs of deliverance" - Psalm 32:7

Night Terror

Psalm 91:5 "<u>You shall not be afraid of the terror by night</u>, or of the arrow that flies by day."

"To trust God in the light is nothing but to trust him in the dark—that is faith" - Charles Spurgeon

Being afraid of the dark is a natural feeling; not being able to see what may be around or approaching us is frightening. Children often feel afraid going to bed at night, even though their parents are in the next room. This is because they cannot see or feel their parents right next to them. They are unable to comprehend that a father or mother would do everything in their power to protect them. As a parent, you try to reassure your children of this, but it usually does not take away their fear. As adults, we sometimes have that same relationship with God. Although He promises in His word over and over again that He is our protector, we are still fearful.

The inside of our Ugandan house consisted of a kitchen, dinning area, living room, three bedrooms, and two bathrooms. The bedroom Edith and her daughter stayed in had a double bed and Carrie and I had bedrooms with single beds. The house was nicer than I expected. It had running water, which we had to boil for cooking to kill any bacteria. My bedroom housed a family of geckos, and Carrie had some cockroaches in her room. There were some holes in the foundation, and we suspected that rats or mice came in and out as they pleased. One day we decided to stuff the holes with paper that we soaked in the bleach-based detergent that we used to wash our towels. The windows in the house had thin metal bars on them and wooden shutters that closed from the inside. We were told that we should keep the shutters closed and locked at night.

It was hot at night, which made it difficult to sleep. We had mosquito nets over our bed that made it even hotter. At the end of our street there was a bar that played music until 2 a.m., and even if I was exhausted, I could not sleep because of the noise. I would finally fall asleep after 2 a.m. but would only sleep until 5:40 a.m. because that was when the Muslim call to prayer blasted throughout our neighborhood. Even if I did fall back to sleep when it was over, I usually had to get up at 6:30 to be on the road by 7:30 or 8:00 in the morning.

One night I was so hot that I slept with the window shutters open. There were some sheer curtains that hung in front of my window. At about 3 a.m., I heard the metal on my window rattling. I got out of bed and peaked out from behind the curtain—there was a shadow of a man standing there. I ran into Edith's room and woke her up. She called Charles, the man who was in charge of taking care of the property and opening up the gate. As it turned out, it was Charles at my window trying to reach in and close my shutters.

One day when we came home from our travels, we saw a large group of people gathered across the street at the small house. Apparently, the father who lived there was killed in a car accident. I told Edith and Carrie that I would like to make a meal and bring it over to the family.

"No, you can't do that," Edith said

"Why not?" I asked. "I think it would be a great way to show the love of Christ to them, especially because they are Muslim."

Edith simply repeated, "No!"

At night, there was a huge gathering of people at the house. I could hear a Muslim religious leader, an Imam, with a microphone/megaphone speaking, but it was not in English. I asked Edith what he was yelling about. She told me the gist of it was that he was yelling at Carrie and me because we were Christians in their neighborhood; he wanted us to leave. This went on all night long until the call for prayer at 5:40 a.m. Concerns over the back gate being unlocked went through my mind a few times, and I had to ask God for protection and believe that He would protect us. He did; nobody approached our house that night.

That was not the last night I was anxious. One night, Carrie was sleeping at an orphanage in the east, and Edith planned to stay at her mom's house because she was sick, so I was in the house alone.

"I can do this," I told myself. "God is my protector, and I will be fine."

I did some laundry and sat outside for a while to read. It was about 5:30, and I was cooking some food on the stove for dinner. All of a sudden, thunder shook the earth and lightning flashed across the sky. The hairs on my arms stood up as there was a flash, and the power went out. I got my headlamp, so I could finish cooking. After dinner, I sat down with my Bible and some devotionals and started reading, because I knew God would reassure me through His word that He was with me. Shortly after my phone rang; it was my daughter calling from the U.S. She asked how I was doing

"I'm okay," I told her "But I am alone in the house with no power, and it is beginning to get dark."

I hated the thought of being stuck in the house with just a flashlight and God only knows how many geckos, bugs, and rodents. My daughter prayed with me, and we talked for a bit. The sky had grown dark by the time we got off the phone. It was hot, but I didn't dare open the windows. So, I sat there in the dark. About thirty minutes later, the power came on.

At 9:00, I heard a knock at the door. I peeked through the window and saw with elation that it was Edith. She told me she did not want me to sleep in the house alone all night, so she left her mom's house. Even though I know that God is my protector, my initial response to the circumstances of all these nights was fear. I could not help the worries and worst-case scenarios that ran through my head, but I knew that I had to immediately take those thoughts captive and not let fear get the best of me. <u>God came through for me once again! He said that I should not be afraid of the terror by night in Psalm 91:5, and He was right!</u>

Reflection

Just like a child usually outgrows their fear of sleeping alone at night once they understand how much their parents love them, an adult can conquer their fears when they comprehend how much they are loved by God. Allowing His Son, Jesus, to take our place and die for our sins, is a type of devotion that I have never witnessed by any human. A person may sacrifice their own life for somebody, but to sacrifice the life of their child for someone else is totally different. What is your biggest fear right now and how are you doing with conquering that fear? These promises from God remind me that I have nothing to worry about:

"Can a mother forget her nursing child? Can she feel no love for the child she has borne? But even if that were possible, I would not forget you! See, I have written your name on the palms of my hands." - Isaiah 49:15-16

"If I say, 'Surely the darkness shall fall on me,' even the night shall be light about me; indeed, the darkness shall not hide from You {God}, but the night shines as the day; the darkness and the light are both alike to You. For you formed my inward parts; You covered me in my mother's womb. I will praise You, for I am fearfully and wonderfully made; marvelous are Your works, and that my soul knows very well. My frame was not hidden from You, when I was made in secret, and skillfully wrought in the lowest parts of the earth. Your eyes saw my substance, being yet unformed. And in Your book they all were written, the days fashioned for me, when as yet there were none of them. How precious also are Your thoughts to me, O God! How great is the sum of them! If I should count them, they would be more in number than the sand." - Psalm 139:11-18

The Enemy Within

Psalm 91:6 "Nor of the pestilence that walks in darkness, nor of the destruction that lays waste at noonday."

"When you are so weak that you cannot do much more than cry, you coin diamonds with both your eyes. The sweetest prayers God ever hears are the groans and sighs of those who have no hope in anything but his love." - Charles Spurgeon

Did you know that God keeps track of the tears we cry? It is written in Psalm 56:8 that our tears are written in His book and stored in His bottle. That is how much He loves us. I will never forget when my daughter was a baby, and I would bring her to the pediatrician to get a vaccination. As he administered the vaccine, she would cry and look at me wondering why I would let this man hurt her. She could not comprehend that this pain was for her good. Our relationship with God works the same way; we often do not understand why He allows suffering in our lives. Sometimes we realize in hindsight that the pain was actually for our good. Yet, there are other times when we still don't know why God allowed the pain. I guess we will have to wait until we see Him face to face to ask Him about those circumstances.

Between July 24 and July 27 there were 122 new cases of Ebola in western Africa. Uganda was almost 3,000 miles away, but the Entebbe Airport was still open. People were coming in and out of Uganda by all different modes of transportation. In fact, when I boarded the plane to leave Uganda at the end of the summer, the stewardesses wore masks and walked up and down the aisles of the plane spraying disinfectant all over us. Thank God I had a sweatshirt on with a hood, and I was able to cover my head and put it down. I totally trusted the Lord to protect me from Ebola in Uganda, and He did! Sometimes, however, God allows certain things to happen to us, not only to heal us, but also to teach us something.

A few years after my trip to Uganda, my daughter was diagnosed with severe Lyme disease. Someone recommended that she see a Kinesiologist. I had been feeling very fatigued for a while and losing weight, so I made an appointment with the Kinesiologist too. Through muscle testing, he was able to tell me that I had some infections and parasites. He prescribed some herbs and probiotics, which I began taking to get rid of both my problems. I started feeling better in a month, and some parasites and eggs began coming out of me. This continued for a while, and after a few months, the Kinesiologist told me that I could stop the herbs. He recommended that I started drinking a beverage that had the reishi mushroom in it, because it would help balance the physiology in my body and boost my immune system.

A few months went by, and I was beginning to feel nauseous when I ate. I stopped the beverage with the mushroom and would drink ginger tea because it helped with the nausea. As the week went on, everything I tried to eat made me nauseous. The only thing that did not was a hard-boiled egg. That weekend, I started getting pain in my head and neck. I took some Tylenol, which helped a little with the pain, but I was still nauseous, and ginger tea was no longer helping. The next day, I had extreme pain and extreme nausea. I took a gram of Tylenol and 800mg of Motrin, but it didn't touch the pain. I had never felt pain like this in my life; I could not do anything, but lay in bed and cry. I couldn't even call an ambulance. As I lay there sobbing, I cried out to God, asking Him why this was happening to me. I prayed that the pain would stop, but it didn't.

I finally cried out hysterically, "God I know that you want good for me and not harm, so this pain must be good for me." I feel asleep shortly after and slept for hours. When I woke up the pain wasn't as bad, so I got up and made some tea. Halfway through the tea, I started feeling pain and had to get back in bed, where I fell back to sleep. I woke up very early the next morning. The pain was fifty-percent better, so I made some toast and had a cup of tea. I took some Tylenol and Motrin, and it helped the pain.

Two days later, I had a bad headache again, as well as stomach pain and muscle aches. I was so weak that I had to lie down. Eventually, I felt like I had to go to the bathroom where I passed a tapeworm—I was horrified!! Since I like my meat well done, and I do not eat sushi or undercooked fish, my doctor thinks I got the tapeworm when I was in Uganda.

I am not sharing this story to gross anyone out, but to say that sometimes when we think God is not answering our prayers, He actually is. The excruciating pain I experienced over that weekend was the die-off of the tapeworm. When they die in your body, they release a lot of toxins. God was trying to have me experience as little pain as possible; that is why I was able to sleep so much. Just like a surgeon cuts to heal, God allowed the pain I felt to rid me of the <u>parasites that were multiplying in the darkness of my body. I had no idea that I had them, but God did, and He took care of them like He promised in Psalm 91:6.</u>

Reflection

Has there ever been a time when you have allowed your child or pet to go through some pain because it was the only way to make them well? Maybe you are currently taking care of an elderly parent who wants to live at home, but it is no longer safe for them to do so. As such, you are causing them emotional pain because they have to say goodbye to their independence and leave their home. Likewise, God's ways are not our ways and His thoughts are not our thoughts (Isaiah 55:8-9) and sometimes we cannot imagine why He allows things to happen to us. However, if we trust that He truly wants what is best for us, then we can have faith that things will be okay. Here are some words that encourage me to trust when I do not understand what is going on:

"Come to Me, all you who labor and are heavy laden, and I will give your rest. Take My yoke upon you and learn from Me, for I am gentle and lowly in heart, and you will find rest for your souls. For My yoke is easy and My burden is light." - Matthew 11:28-29

"For I know the plans I have for you, declares the Lord, plans to prosper you and not to harm you, plans to give you hope and a future. Then you will call on me and come and pray to me, and I will listen to you. You will seek me and find me when you seek me with all your heart." - Jeremiah 29:11

Kasese

Psalm 91:7-8 "A thousand may fall at your side, and ten thousand at your right hand; <u>but it shall not come near to you</u> Only with your eyes shall you look and see the reward of the wicked."

"Our faith must be built on strong determined confidence in God." - Oswald Chambers

To be "determined" is to make a firm decision in which you do not waver. The Bible states that doubting is like a wave being tossed back and forth by the wind (James 1:6). How does one arrive at the place where they are absolutely certain about something? One way is through constant reassurance. If I feed my kids every day they have not doubt that I will provide food for them tomorrow. Similarly, God builds our faith by allowing trials in our lives. When I was diagnosed with cancer, I decided to trust God and accept the outcome— However, I believed He would heal me. Leaving my future totally in His hands was so freeing—I learned to trust and persevere, while God encouraged and guided me. Through this experience and other tribulations, He showed me that His promises are true. Therefore, I became confident in God's ability to protect me in a life-threatening situation. As such, I was able to advance towards possible danger rather than retreat.

When we traveled to eastern Uganda to visit the CURE hospital, Carrie and I chose a hotel that had Wi-Fi. I was eager to check my emails; because it was the first time I had access to Wi-Fi since I landed in Uganda. I had received an email two hours earlier from the US embassy in Kampala. There was an attack in Kasese, which is in western Uganda; militia from the Congo killed eighty-eight civilians. We were scheduled to be in Kasese in two weeks to visit schools for the deaf in that area. The embassy was warning Americans that the terror threat was high, and we needed to be cautious and stay away from religious institutions, malls, restaurants, public transportation, and hotels throughout Uganda. There was no way we could avoid these places while continuing on our expedition, so we put our trust in the Lord.

We had been back from the East for a week, and we were seeking God for confirmation that He still wanted us to go to Kasese. We had appointments with a couple of schools for the deaf, and we decided to put a fleece out – which is asking God to do something to prove His will. In the Bible, Gideon did this in Judges 6:36-40. Our "fleece" was that we were not going to call the schools to confirm our appointments, but if the schools called us to confirm, we would go to Kasese. It appeared that God was opening the door for us to go, because the day before our appointments the schools called to confirm.

On the way to Kasese, we stopped and visited a school for the deaf, and the visit was very fruitful. The countryside driving to the West was beautiful! We found a hotel in Busheyni and I was awake all night, because the mattress and pillow were as hard as a rock. I thought of Jesus and His disciples going around the countryside, ministering to people and at night sleeping on the ground outside; I suddenly became very grateful to be indoors. In the morning, we were back on the road. We drove for a few hours to visit another school about ninety minutes from Kasese. When we arrived in Kasese, we were tired, but we needed to find a hotel to stay in: one that we could afford and would feel safe in. It took us a while to find one, but it was a nice hotel. The beds and pillows were comfortable, the food was great, there was Wi-Fi, air conditioning, and an armed guard at the door of the hotel.

We had finished our work and Edith thought it would be nice for us to go on a safari, so the next day we drove to Queen Elizabeth National Park., which borders the Congo. We saw all kinds of animals: lions, antelope, buffalo, elephants, monkeys, wort hogs, hippos, a leopard, and many types of deer-like animals. It was amazing to see the animals in their natural environment running loose. It was a wonderful day, and I really felt that God blessed us with the beauty of His creation, because we were obedient to what He called us to do. We got safely back to our house on the outskirts of Kampala, and a couple of weeks later we heard that there was another attack in Kasese, and more people died. <u>Our commanding</u>

officer got us in and out of Kasese safely; there were no attacks when we were there.

It has been five years since I was in Uganda. I heard on the news a few months ago that an American woman was in Queen Elizabeth National Park with her driver when four armed men approached the car and kidnapped her. The kidnappers were from the Congo, just like it was militia from the Congo who killed the civilians a couple of weeks before we got there in 2014. The woman was let go five days later. The news never mentioned if the ransom the men were demanding was paid. This confirmed to me that God truly protected me, as stated in Psalm 91:7-8, while I was in Kasese and in Queen Elizabeth National Park.

Reflection

A person in the armed forces has to go through extensive training before they are thrown into a combat situation. This is for a number of reasons: they need to learn how to obey orders, trust their commanding officer, and their team members. I had been on other mission trips prior to Africa and each deployment brought me to a new level of total reliance on God. Instead of thinking about the warnings from the US Embassy, I was focusing on my team's assignment and doing what I needed to do. When the enemy tried to instill fear, I thought about all the times God came through for me. These are some words that encourage me when I am facing possible danger and decide to move forward anyway:

"The Lord watches over you—the Lord is your shade at your right hand; the sun will not harm you by day, or the moon by night. The Lord will keep you from all harm—he will watch over your life; the LORD will watch over your coming and going both now and forevermore" - Psalm 121: 5-8

"I give them eternal life, and they shall never perish; no one will snatch them out of my hand" - John 10:28-30

Venturing Out Alone

Psalm 91:9-10 "Because you have made the Lord, who is my refuge, Even the Most High, your dwelling place, <u>No evil shall befall you,</u> nor shall any plague come near your dwelling."

"He who is not everyday conquering some fear has not learned <u>the secret of life.</u>" - Ralph Waldo Emerson

That quote is so true; it is in fearful situations that our faith and trust in God grows stronger. My daughter was very cautious as a child. Like most children, she took her first step right into my arms. Each time she tried to walk, I would move a little farther away from her, causing her to take more steps. Eventually, she could walk on her own and explore the house, which meant I had to watch her more carefully and know where she was at all times. If I could not do that, I would put her in a playpen where she would be safe. Although it was easier for me to have her in a secure place, it was better for her to experience new things and have the freedom to wander. When I felt she was capable of playing in the yard while I was in the house, I let her. She went outside, because she was confident that if she yelled for me, I would be right there. Likewise, when we realize that God will help us when we cry out to Him, we become free to explore and experience all that He has for us in this world. This allows us to move forward without worrying about danger or disease. For me, <u>the secret of life</u> is freedom from bondage and being who God created me to be.

The longer I was in Uganda, the more comfortable I became with my surroundings. Sometimes I actually slept with my bedroom window open. I felt comfortable sitting on a chair in the yard reading a book, knowing that the back gate was unlocked. After church on Sundays, we would go to a restaurant in Kampala that had American-style food. Next to the restaurant were a few stores, and I would go to one store to get supplies, while Carrie and Edith would go to another store. One time, Adolf was driving Carrie and me to the mall that was in downtown Kampala in heavy traffic. The mall wasn't too far away, so Carrie and I got out and walked to the mall while Adolf continued driving to the spot where he met us after we were done shopping. We split up at the mall and were on different floors shopping to save time. I was told by someone who traveled to Africa frequently that a white woman could not safely walk around in Kampala by herself. Truly, the Lord had a hedge of protection around us. Sometimes our plan of operation caused our team to be separated. On a few other occasions, I was in the car alone with Adolph going to factories, outside markets, and schools for the deaf.

Carrie decided to spend a couple of days at an orphanage in Jinja, so Adolf drove her there and stayed in Jinja. He arranged for somebody else to be our driver while they were away. During that time, Edith and I were meeting with different doctors at the Mulago Hospital in Kampala to determine what they needed to successfully perform cochlear implant surgery. They not only lacked equipment, they also requested that someone come to Uganda and teach them how to use it. On our way home we were driving through the city of Kampala during rush hour, when our automobile broke down in the middle of the busy street. The driver got out and told us to stay put, as he walked away.

We did not really know the man and Edith and I were stuck in the car with vehicles passing us on both sides. This was definitely a time when we needed protection and reinforcements. Anyone could have approached us, or we could have caused an accident. This would not be such a big deal in America, because even if we were in an unsafe part of a city, we could call a roadside service or the police. However, those choices were not an option in Uganda. Edith called Adolf and he and Carrie were on their way home from Jinja and only about forty-five minutes away from us. God is so good; Adolf picked us up, and we all got back to our house safely. <u>God's promises came alive for us once again; no evil touched us,</u> as promised in Psalm 91:9-10.

Reflection

Have you learned the secret of life? If not, what fears are keeping you in bondage. We all have something that scares us, so it is important to remember who instigates that fear. It is not God, because he did not give us a spirit of fear; He gives us a spirit "of power, and of love and of a sound mind" (2 Timothy 1:7). As such, do not let the enemy prevent you from fulfilling your purpose in life. The first scripture below is the one that God gave me when He called me to the mission field; it was there that I was set free from the fear of man. The other scripture is how I was set free from the fear of death:

"Eye has not seen, nor ear heard, nor have entered into the heart of man the things which God has prepared for those who love Him. But God has revealed them to us through His Spirit." - 1 Corinthians 2:9

"Therefore, there is now no condemnation for those who are in Christ Jesus, because through Christ Jesus the law of the Spirit who gives life has set you free from the law of sin and death. For what the law was powerless to do because it was weakened by the flesh, God did by sending his own Son in the likeness of sinful flesh to be a sin offering. And so he condemned sin in the flesh, in order that the righteous requirement of the law might be fully met in us, who do not live according to the flesh but according to the Spirit." - Romans 8:1-4

Boldness

Psalm 91:11-12 "For He shall give His angels charge over you, to keep you in all your ways. In their hands they shall bear you up, lest you dash your foot against a stone."

"If what we call love, doesn't take us beyond ourselves, it is not really love." - Oswald Chambers

There are many different kinds of love and ulterior motives for it. The love that Oswald Chambers referenced in his quote is sacrificial love, which causes a person to forget about themselves, their safety, or their desires because their focus is on the well-being of others. If you are married or you have children, you truly understand this type of love. As such, you are more likely to know the depth of God's love for you. His word tells us that we can do all kinds of great deeds and charity work, but if we do not do them in love, it profits nothing (1 Corinthians 13:1-3). This means that if I perform some humanitarian act to look good to my boss and do not really care about the people I am helping, I will not get rewarded for it in Heaven. When I went on my first mission trip, I had no idea how I would feel about the children. I had compassion for them, but how could I love someone I never met before? I prayed on the plane that God will fill me with His love for the people of Mexico and He did. It was His love inside of me that made me want to do whatever I could for the children in Uganda.

We had not planned to refurnish the dorm rooms in any of the schools for the deaf. As such, we did not come prepared with plans or funds to complete this type of project. However, as we spent time at one of the schools with the children, we saw that their living conditions were awful. We decided that we would contact people in America for the money to get these children what they needed. The organization, Good Samaritan Mission Council, that processed the donations for our trip to Uganda, sent us a check for the whole project when they heard about the needs at the school. They truly are the reason we were able to bless these children!

God proved His goodness time and time again; the donation we received was enough money for us to buy paint, beds, mattresses, sheets, blankets, and mosquito nets for the children's rooms. We were also able to buy a sprayer and bug spray, so that we could get rid of the bed bugs in the concrete walls. The children went home for school vacation, so we took all the torn foam mattresses and ripped blankets out the dorms; washed the walls and floors with bleach; sprayed the walls; and did some painting.

On the day we went to pick up the mattresses and beds in Kampala, we dropped Edith off to get the kids some Bibles in another part of the city. Adolf drove Carrie, Edith's daughter, and me to meet the man we hired to bring all the new beds and mattresses to the dorms. He followed us across the city and when we arrived at the store, God blessed us with a parking space right in front. All the beds for sale were outside on the grass, and there was a small structure for the office in the back. As we walked around and picked out the beds we wanted to buy, I noticed that the beds lacked paint in some areas. I told the man helping us that I would not buy any beds unless he painted the spots, so he agreed to spray paint them. The man we hired with the truck went to find a spot to park in the city until the beds were ready.

Adolf walked up the street to have lunch, while we stayed in the car and waited for the beds to be painted. Suddenly, the owner of the store started knocking on the window telling me to move the car, because he needed the parking spot. I cracked the window and told him that I couldn't move the car. He started yelling, and people in the busy street were stopping and looking at us. Well, God gave me the strength and boldness I needed to deal with the situation. I got out of the car and told Carrie to lock the doors. I told the storeowner that my driver went to lunch, and I did not have a license to drive in Uganda. Nevertheless, he kept yelling. At this point, my Italian descent kicked in, and I stood my ground. I told him that he could yell all he wanted to, but I was NOT moving the car. I was still a customer because I did not have the beds yet, and I was staying there until the beds were done being painted. Then I got back in the car and locked the door. He eventually walked away and so did the spectators. I think he was shocked that a white woman stood up to him. He evidently never encountered an Italian Christian woman with the power of the Holy Spirit in her.

The beds were ready shortly after Adolf returned from lunch. The man we hired drove to the store and loaded the beds on his truck. We picked Edith up on our way to the school. By the time we got there, it was 4:00 in the afternoon. After the beds and mattresses were unloaded from the truck and put in the dorms, we started putting sheets, a blanket, a mosquito net, and a Bible on each of the beds. When we finished, it looked awesome, and the teachers were blown away. No words could explain the joy that I had, knowing that these beautiful children had what they needed! When I read verses 11 and 12 of Psalm 91, I still think of that day, because <u>I was tired, fearful, and outnumbered; however, I felt like I had an army behind me to come to my aid, if I needed it. Even though I couldn't see the angels encamped around me like they were around Elisha when the Syrians were about to attack in 2 Kings 6:16-18, I knew they were there. Afterall, my heavenly Father was watching out for me, just like I watched out for my daughter.</u> The promises in Psalm 91:11-12 came true.

Reflection

Although we had the money to buy all the items we needed to refurnish the dorms, we were still met with opposition while trying to complete our mission. The enemy did not want these children to be safe from mosquitos or have any type of comfort. He tried to instill fear in me through the store owner. God only knows what would have happened if I moved the car. If you are dealing with some contention in your life right now, here are some words that encouraged me and gave me strength to accomplish what I needed to do:

"God has said, never will I leave you; never will I forsake you. So we say with confidence, The Lord is my helper; I will not be afraid. What can mere mortals do to me?" - Hebrews 13:5-6 NIV

"And my God shall supply all your need according to His riches in glory by Christ Jesus." - Philippians 4:19

Snakes

Psalm 91:13 "You shall tread upon the lion and the cobra, the young lion and the serpent you shall trample underfoot."

"You gain strength, courage and confidence by every experience in which you really stop to look fear in the face. You are able to say to yourself, I have lived through this horror, I can take the next thing that comes along. You must do the thing you think you cannot do." - Eleanor Roosevelt

    We all have fears, but sometimes we cannot imagine why some people are afraid of certain things. I have relatives who are afraid to fly, but that is not an issue for me; however, they bravely face their fear and fly anyway. We cannot let fear be the determining factor of where we go or what we do in life. If we allow it to penetrate us, it takes root and spreads. The quote above truly sums up my fear of snakes. Each experience I had in Uganda where I could have encounter one was scarier than the previous time. God tends to do this in order to build our trust in Him. Before I left for Africa, I would occasionally see little garden snakes in my yard and eventually my fear of them became minimal. However, there are some seriously huge and dangerous serpents in Uganda. Even somebody that likes them may be afraid to come across one unexpectantly in their travels.

    God is definitely aware of my feelings about snakes! In fact, it may have been my biggest fear about going to Africa. When we traveled to southern Uganda, we spent some time in a town called Jinja, which is on the shore of Lake Victoria. That is where the Nile River actually starts. At one point we had to drive onto a ferry and take it across the water. While were waiting for the ferry to arrive, we got out of the car, and I began to talk to some of the people there. I was told that one of the workers was out of work because a green mamba snake had bitten him—only shortly after he had recovered from a cobra bite! There was a clearing where the ferry docked, but on either side of the clearing, there was grass. Apprehension permeated me as we made our way to the ferry—my heart was racing. I kept thinking that even if we made it onto the ferry safely, there was danger of the ferry capsizing. I had to keep telling myself that God would protect me. We boarded the ferry when it arrived, and we crossed safely.

The owner of the school for the deaf, where we remodeled the dorms, wanted us to drive north of Kampala one day to pray over some land he owned. It was his desire to move the school out of the city, but he needed someone to fund the project. I had promised my family that I would not travel to northern Uganda because there was fighting going on there. Since we were only driving a couple of hours north, I decided it was safe to go.

When we arrived at his land, there was a small house on it that he rented out to a family. Behind it there was a large hill on which he wanted us to pray. There was no path, so we would have to climb the hill thorough close-knit cornstalks. I asked if they had seen any snakes recently on the property, and the renter of the house said they killed a baby python the week before, but never saw the mother. This information was more terrifying than the statement I heard at the ferry. I cannot really say I prayed, it was more like I *begged* God that we would not encounter any snakes. As we began our climb up the hill, I realized that the ground was covered in thick crabgrass; there was no way to see what was under it, and I was petrified. I began to focus on scriptures, especially Joshua 1:9 that says to be strong and courageous and not afraid, because God is always with me. When we were halfway to the top we came to a tiny clearing. I asked if we could pray there, instead of climbing the rest of the way; sensing my fear, the owner agreed. I think that was the first time I ever prayed without closing my eyes. I could not get down the hill fast enough. We made it down safely without seeing Mamma Python—once again, God protected me from my biggest fear.

The night I was flying home from Uganda, Carrie and I ate at a hotel restaurant in Kampala. As it was beginning to get dark, the host walked us down a path in the back of the hotel that was lit with torches. There were sporadic tables, bushes, and trees around us; the landscaping was beautiful, but I had no idea what was lurking in the surroundings. The woman who arranged for Adolf to be our driver told me that when she was in Uganda there was a black mamba snake in one of the hotels in the city. I asked Carrie if we could eat inside, but she really wanted to eat outside. It was my last night there, and I chose to face my fear in order to enjoy my surroundings. We made it through without seeing a serpent. When I think about my experiences, traveling through grasslands, hills, riverbanks, and hiking Sipi Falls, there were snakes all around me; <u>I treaded upon the cobra and I was safe,</u> just as Psalm 91:13 promised. To this day, I still thank God that I didn't have to "trample" them under my feet!

Reflection

Because I lived through the horror of climbing the hill with the cornstalks, I gained more confidence and trust in God. I was able to enjoy my dinner outside at the hotel. What snake in your life are you facing? Is it keeping you from experiencing the things you would like to do? If so, you are being robbed of an adventure. When Jesus walked on this earth, He told His follows, "The thief does not come except to steal, and kill, and to destroy. I have come that they may have life, and that they may have it more abundantly" (John 10:10). Satan is that thief, he wants to steal all your joy, but God wants you to have abundant life. Whose voice are you going to listen to? The choice is yours! The scriptures below encourage me to keep going when I am facing fear:

"Fear not, for I have redeemed you; I have called you by your name; You are Mine. When you pass through the waters, I will be with you; and when you pass through the rivers, they will not sweep over you. When you walk through the fire, you shall not be burned, nor shall the flame scorch you. For I am the Lord your God." - Isaiah 43:1-3

"Be strong and courageous. Do not be afraid or terrified because of them, for the Lord your God goes with you: he will never leave you or forsake you." - Deuteronomy 3:16

Leaving Uganda – the Airport

Psalm 91:14-15 "Because he has set his love upon Me, therefore I will deliver him; I will set him on high, because he has known My name. He shall call upon Me, and I will answer him; I will be with him in trouble; I will deliver him and honor him"

"Prayer in private results in boldness in public." - Edwin Louis Cole

    I can be very blunt when talking to people—I tell it like it is. I often wondered why I had this trait and would blame it on my Italian descent. However, God showed me that he created me with that characteristic in my personality because He wanted to use it for His purpose. The Bible says in 1 Corinthians 12:12 that our bodies have many parts: arms, legs, eyes, and so on. We couldn't function as people if some of us only had eyes and others only had legs. God considers his children one body in Christ. As such, we have different personalities and gifts. When a group of people with different gifts work together, they can accomplish mighty things.

    It was my last day in Africa, and my time there had flown by so quickly; I had mixed emotions about leaving. The people of Uganda are loving, self-sacrificing, generous, and have unbelievable faith! However, I missed my family and friends, as well as some of the comforts that come with living in America. After Carrie and I ate dinner, I went up to Carrie's hotel room and took a nice hot shower before heading to the airport. Carrie was flying to New York the next day on a different airline. Adolf picked me up at 11:00 p.m. to bring me to the Entebbe Airport. Driving there, I was wondering why I had chosen a flight that was leaving Uganda at 1:10 am. Of course, I knew that it was the only flight that this airline offered to America, via London, but on my way to the airport I starting getting a little nervous. I had no idea what to expect when I got there, or how many people would be there that late at night. I felt similar to the way I had when I got off the plane in Uganda, but my confidence had increased. The difference was that God had been so faithful to protect me and answer my prayers over the summer that my faith was stronger than ever.

When I got to the airport, there were hardly any people inside, and it was pretty easy to navigate my way around. When I turned a corner, I could see a line of people waiting to go through customs, mostly white men. When it was my turn, I gave the customs officer my airline ticket, passport, and visa. He perused the documents, then looked up and said that there was no date stamped on my visa, so he couldn't let me go through. Of all things, I never expected this.

"What do you mean??!" I asked.

Evidently, the customs officer who had dealt with me when I arrived in Uganda never stamped the visa he gave me. The officer told me that I had to go to the US Embassy and straighten out the situation.

"I can't go the embassy, its closed and even if it was open, I have no way of getting there!" I stated.

"There is nothing I can do about it and you need to get out of line" he said.

When I looked behind me there was a long line of people—I said to myself, "God, please help me!" Well, my Italian boldness kicked into action.

"There is no way that I am leaving this line", I firmly stated.

Suddenly, I remembered that I still had my airline ticket from my flight to Uganda. I got it out of my carry-on bag and showed him the ticket and luggage tags sure that this was proof that I came into the country on that date. He said that I still had to go the embassy because my visa had no stamp. The line behind me was really long at this point and a man who worked at the airport came over to see what the problem was. I told him what was going on and showed him my airline ticket to Uganda. He told the customs officer to let me through. I found my way to the gate and sat down, at this point I had a myriad of feelings going on: quivers, relief, anger, and gratefulness. It's funny how the anxiety did not kick in until after I made it through customs. I was so busy arguing with the customs officer that I was not even afraid at the time. I guess God really knew what He was doing when He called me to go on this mission trip. He knew I would need the spirit of boldness that He created within me.

I was no longer sad to be leaving Uganda; in fact, I could not wait to get on the plane. When I landed in London, I had a nine-hour layover, and my phone was not working. At first, I was dreading the long wait, because I just wanted to get home. I knew at that point what someone in the military must feel like at the end of their deployment. Luckily, Heathrow Airport has tons of things to do. I had some delicious gluten-free food and did some shopping. After hours of exploring the airport, I discovered a candy store that had the best gluten-free chocolate and there was a woman there who showed me how to reset my phone. I sent my daughter and Carrie a quick message, saying I had arrived in London safely.

When I got on the plane to America, I reflected on my journey. I realized that the long layover at Heathrow Airport was just what I needed to destress before I arrived home. Once again God's promises came true for me. When <u>I called upon Him for help, he gave me courage. He reminded me of my airplane ticket to Uganda. He sent a man to see what the commotion was and helped me get through customs. God also set me on high and honored me because I set my love upon Him</u>, just like He promises in Psalm 91:14-15!

Reflection

There are so many good things that people can accomplish when they work together as one body. Edith's great faith, knowledge of the terrain, and understanding of the challenges the deaf children in Uganda face daily, were essential for our mission to be a success. Carrie's expertise in sign language, her sweet spirit, and joy were a constant reminder to stay positive. When we would arrive home, tired and hungry, after a long day, Carrie would still be dancing around the house with Edith's five-year-old daughter, singing songs from *The Sound of Music*. As you can see from my stories, I had the medical knowledge, the boldness to accomplish what needed to be done, and the desire to pray about everything. I am not saying that it was always easy for us to work as a team; but with God as our leader all things were possible, as long as our eyes were on Him and not our circumstances. Whether I was with my team or traveling alone, prayer was the key to my success. When Jesus was on this earth he said, "Ask, and it will be given to you; seek, and you will find; knock, and it will be opened to you. For everyone who asks receives and he who seeks finds and to him who knocks it will be opened. Or what man is there among you who, if his son asks for bread, will give him a stone: Or if he asks for a fish, will give him a serpent? If you then, being evil, know how to give good gifts to your children, how much more will your Father who is in heaven give good things to those who ask Him!" (Matthew 7:7-11).The scriptures below sum up what God did for me at the airport when I was leaving Uganda. They are also good promises from God to focus on if you find yourself blindsided by something:

"No weapon formed against you shall prosper, and every tongue which rises against you in judgment You shall condemn. This is the heritage of the servants of the Lord" - Isaiah 54:17

"On the day I called, You answered me; You made me bold with strength in my soul." - Psalm 138:3

Fruits of My Labor

Psalm 91:16 "With long life I will satisfy him and show him My salvation."

"I expect to pass through life but once. If therefore, there be any kindness I can show, or any good thing I can do to any fellow being, let me do it now, and not defer or neglect it, as I shall not pass this way again." - William Penn

    Sometimes when God calls us to do something, we see immediate results. Yet, other times it takes years before we see a vision become reality. I worked hard to get equipment and doctors to go to Uganda after I returned home from my trip. Getting some equipment was possible, but I could not find a doctor willing to travel to Uganda to train the surgeons, or a technician willing to teach the doctors how to use the equipment. After a year, I realized that God was not opening the door for me to accomplish what I wanted to do. The Bible says in 1 Corinthians 3:7 "Neither the one who plants nor the one who waters is anything, but only God, who makes things grow." My job was sowing seeds. By visiting schools and hospitals to see what was available, I was able to discern what was needed to help these precious deaf children get cochlear implants. You see, God had somebody else in mind to find the doctors, get the equipment, and start a school. It was actually a couple from another country that made this dream a reality. Three and a half years after I left Uganda, two deaf children were able to have cochlear implant surgery. The next year, a school and rehab center was opened for deaf children. In January of 2019, Carrie went back to Uganda to teach and set up a curriculum for the school. Although they wanted me to return to Uganda as well, I was unable to go because I was sick.
    In the fall of 2018, I began losing a lot of weight, and I had extreme joint pain in my neck, shoulders, arms, and hips. I went to the doctors for a checkup, and my blood work came back positive for Lupus; however, that diagnosis did not explain the weight loss. Since I had cancer in the past, my doctor ordered a series of tests on different parts of my body

to see if there was cancer anywhere, but everything came back fine. In the meantime, I went to see a Rheumatologist, who ran more in-depth tests, and I was diagnosed with a condition called Polymyalgia Rheumatica. A bone scan also showed that I had osteoporosis in my spine and hips. God gave me a promise when I was diagnosed with cancer that is in Psalm 92:14; it says, "They shall still bear fruit in old age; they shall be fresh and flourishing." Currently, I am in remission with my cancer and my autoimmune disease.

Psalm 91:16 came true for not only me, but also the children in Uganda: For me, my time on earth is not over yet. For the deaf children in Uganda, a whole new life is beginning for them. <u>They will no longer have a long life of suffering and abuse; instead they will be able to communicate with their families, hear the laughter of their friends, and God's word of salvation</u>!

Reflection

I pray that this book has given you a glimpse of how faithful and loving God really is. If I truly think of Him as my Father or my commanding officer, I can understand His ways better. However, there are things I may never understand until I ask Him in Heaven. One thing I am certain of, is that He has a plan for your life and so does the enemy of your soul. This fact should not cause you to be afraid, it should make you realize that you are in a spiritual battle, but you can win that battle, because God is more powerful than Satan. I lived out Psalm 91 while I was in Uganda and so did the soldiers of the 91st Brigade in World War I. This tells me that you can too, if you believe in God the Father, Jesus the Son, and the Holy Spirit.

Everyone is aware of the rapid passage of time, yet we still tend to put things off that we have a passion for, because we believe we have to plan for the future and get everything in order before we venture out to try something new. However, now more than ever, the world seems unstable. Pandemics, tornadoes, wildfires, and earthquakes—the list goes on and on. I had put off writing this book for a while when I heard a pastor say, "If you were to die today, what would you regret not doing?" My first thought was that I would regret that I never wrote my book. What would your regret be?

I hope the scriptures below encourage you to persevere. When that final day comes for you, I pray that you have no regrets, as well as no fear, because you know where you are going after this life!

"We have this treasure in earthen vessels, that the excellence of the power may be of God and not of us. We are hard-pressed on every side, yet not crushed; we are perplexed, but not in despair, persecuted, but not forsaken; struck down but not destroyed." - 2 Corinthians 4:7-9

"For I am persuaded that neither death nor life, nor angels nor principalities nor powers, nor things present, nor things to come, nor height nor depth, nor any other credited thing, shall be able to separate us from the love of God which is in Christ Jesus our Lord." - Romans 8:38-39

Epilogue

Edith and Eddie's vision was fulfilled; their ministry, Hear His Voice, is doing great things and helping so many deaf children in Uganda! Carrie is back in America, making a difference in the lives of deaf children here. Upon my return from Uganda, I have been working as a tutor; I love sowing into the lives of children and helping them attain their academic goals. However, with the coronavirus causing death and destruction throughout the country I love, I feel like I need to be on the frontline somewhere helping.

I have been asking God why I can't be out there making a difference, and this morning when I was praying about it, He reminded me of the Apostle Paul. Paul was not one of Jesus' original disciples, but he became one as he spread the gospel abroad to the gentiles. He was extremely dedicated and effective in spreading the gospel. However, this came to an end when he was imprisoned in Rome. One would wonder why God allowed this to happen? Evidently it was because God had bigger plans for Paul; he wrote half of the New Testament in the Bible while in jail. Paul finished his work on the mission field, and God wanted him to write about his experiences, so that people could be encouraged throughout the ages.

When God called me to write, over a year ago, I started a book about conquering fear. I have gone through many trials throughout my life, and God has always been there for me. My trials have included a miscarriage, divorce, my dad and second husband dying weeks apart, my diagnosis of cancer, my daughter almost dying at age sixteen from a rare illness, being out of work for a couple of years, and having no place to call home for a year. While I was writing about overcoming your fears, I felt a strong desire to start writing a devotional on Psalm 91. I believe that God gave me that desire because He knew that the coronavirus was coming, and He wanted people to know that He is still with them. Since the battle is not over and I am still in the fight, my next mission is to finish my book on fear. I hope that you will join me as I share about my other mission trips, my healings, my losses, my finances, and my miracles. Until then, my prayer for you is that you will "have the power to understand, as all God's people should, how wide, how long, how high, and how deep His love is." - Ephesians 3:18

Photos

*This was our neighborhood.
Our house was behind the wall on the right.*

My bedroom

Sipi Falls

The boys' dorm when we arrived
Two to three boys were sleeping in one twin bunk bed

The truck leaving the store with the beds and mattresses

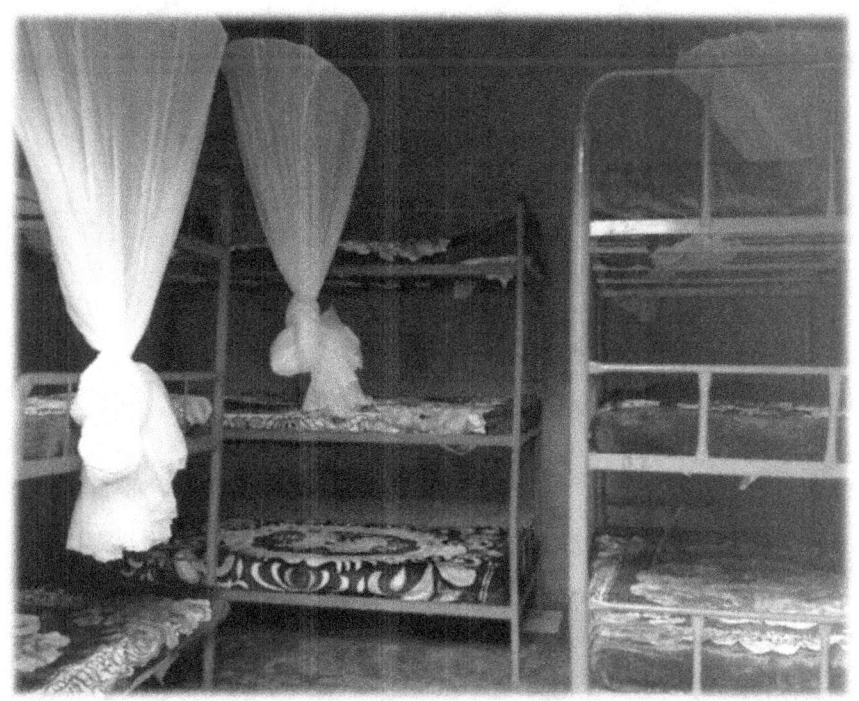
The boys' dorm after our remodel

In GOD We Trust — Psalm 91

1 He who dwells in the shelter of the Most High
will rest in the shadow of the Almighty.
2 I will say of the LORD, "He is my refuge
and fortress, my God, in whom I trust."
3 Surely He will save you from the fowler's snare
and from the deadly pestilence.
4 He will cover you with His feathers,
and under His wings you will find refuge;
His faithfulness will be your shield and rampart.
5 You will not fear the terror of night,
nor the arrow that flies by day,
6 nor the pestilence that stalks in the darkness,
nor the plague that destroys at midday.
7 A thousand may fall at your side, ten thousand
at your right hand, but it will not come near you.
8 You will only observe with your eyes and
see the punishment of the wicked.
9 If you make the Most High your dwelling—
even the LORD, who is your refuge—
10 then no harm will befall you,
no disaster will come near your tent.
11 For He will command His angels concerning
you to guard you in all your ways;
12 they will lift you up in their hands, so that
you will not strike your foot against a stone.
13 You will tread upon the lion and the cobra;
you will trample the great lion and the serpent.
14 "Because he loves me," says the LORD,
"I will rescue him; I will protect him,
for he acknowledges my name.
15 He will call upon me, and I will answer him;
I will be with him in trouble,
I will deliver him and honor him.
16 With long life I will satisfy him
and show him my salvation."

The front of the card given to me when I left for Uganda

Soldiers' Psalm

Psalm 91 is called the Soldier's Psalm. We are told that in World War I, there was a brigade that recited Psalm 91 daily. As word got out, they were nicknamed the "91st Brigade" by other soldiers. This brigade engaged in three of the war's bloodiest battles. Other units suffered up to 90% casualties, but the "91st Brigade" did not suffer a single combat-related death. There are more recent stories of soldiers using Psalm 91 that we are unable to share for security reasons. God is willing and able to keep His words of covenant promise. Plead God's Psalm 91 shield daily. Confidently claim His rest, refuge, safety, covering, faithfulness, freedom from fear, angelic watchers, deliverance, and protection.

Prayer is the War.
God's Word is the Weapon.

The Father's Business
P. O. Box 380333
Birmingham, AL 35238 USA
www.thefathersbusiness.com
©2015 Sylvia Gunter

The back of the card given to me when I left for Uganda

Acknowledgments

Stacy Padula O'Halloran, my precious daughter, friend, and great blessing from God, I cannot imagine life without you. Thank you for supporting my decision to go to Africa and never doubting that God was calling me there. You are such an inspiration in so many ways. Writing a book is a lot more work than I thought. Thank you so much for all your encouragement and guidance; without it, I may never have finished this book! Love you so much!

Mackenzie Wells, thank you for editing my book and also designing the cover. You are so gifted, and I know God has huge plans for your many talents. I have enjoyed our talks and getting to know you!

Edith and Eddie Mukaaya and Carrie Broiller, thank you for allowing me to play a small part in bringing your vision, Hear His Voice, into fruition. Edith and Carrie, I developed such a deep bond and love for you through our adventures in Uganda, and I treasure our relationship. I am so grateful that God crossed our paths!

Adolf Mwesigye, thank you for not only driving me all over Uganda, but also being a protector, friend, and an amazing brother in the Lord. Your faith and strength to persevere through hardships is such a witness for God, and you are a blessing to those who know you!

John and Cindy Norton, you played such a big part in preparing me for Uganda. The time you spent mentoring me in the ways of the African culture and also spiritually, were instrumental to the success of my trip. I actually felt your prayers when I was in Uganda. I loved our lunches and times together, and I am so grateful for both of you!

Bob Beck, thank you for keeping track of the donations for our trip and for sending funds from your own organization, so that we could get the children what they needed for their dorms. You and your organization are a great example of Christianity in action. May you get back tenfold for all that you do to bless others!

I would also like to thank all the generous people that financially supported my trip (there are too many to mention); without the funds, I never would have been able to go. I especially want to thank my family members that did not want me to go, but gave me money anyway, because they knew how important it was to me. A big thank you to my cousins Paul and Sandy, who had a huge welcome home cookout at their house when I returned to the states. I am truly blessed with the most amazing family, and I love you all!

I am extremely grateful to all the people who prayed for me daily, because I know the power of prayer. It was your prayers that strengthened me and kept me safe while I was in Africa. I love you all—God bless you!

Even though we never met, I would like to thank Katie Davis, author of "Kisses from Katie." I read your book before I left for Africa, and it showed me that if I step out in faith I can accomplish so much; that God will be with me; and that a woman can fly to Uganda alone and make a difference in God's kingdom. I was so blessed to be able to visit Amazima while I was in Jinja. Katie, I hope you realize what an inspiration you are to others, and the huge impact you make on God's Kingdom.

Last but not least, a very special thanks to my dear friends Cheryl Adamopoulos, Sandy Forsythe, and Tara Payton, who never doubted that God called me to Africa. You prayed with me, encouraged me, and stood by me, even when other people thought I was crazy to go to Uganda. I love you guys, and I am so very thankful for you!

About the Author

Debra Fredette has always loved working with children. While hers were growing up, she volunteered as a room mother at the elementary school and taught Sunday school. Her church did not have a youth group, so she started one for children in grades 7-12. She ran the youth group for seven years and taught the kids the importance of serving in the community and in homeless shelters.

Debra has had many different professions. She worked as a plan administrator for a financial institution for over five years. Since the medical field always fascinated her, she decided to go back to school to become a certified surgical technologist and then went on to earn her Bachelor of Science degree. After many years of working in the operating room, she had to leave because of a family illness. She was offered a job as an adjunct professor at a junior college and worked there for three years as a clinical instructor and lab teacher. In 2009 she committed to be the director of the surgical technology program for a year.

In 2010, Debra decided to put her love for children and her experience in the medical field together. She traveled as a missionary to Mexico, Haiti, and the Dominican Republic, and she also spent the summer of 2014 in Africa. Upon returning to the states, she decided to continue her work with children as a tutor and substitute teacher. She enjoys tutoring a variety of subjects, standardized tests, and college admission essays.

www.ingramcontent.com/pod-product-compliance
Lightning Source LLC
Chambersburg PA
CBHW070119110526
44587CB00015BA/2647